CHRIS_TOMLIN
BURNING_LIGHTS_ _

THE CHORAL COLLECTION
Arranged & Orchestrated by Cliff Duren

AVAILABLE PRODUCTS:

Choral Book	45757-2285-7
CD Preview Pak	45757-2285-1
Listening CD	45757-2285-2
Split-Track Accompaniment CD	45757-2285-3
Audio .Wav Files DVD-Rom	45757-2285-4
(Praise Band/Strings/Brass)	
Orchestration/Conductor's Score CD-Rom	45757-2285-8
Rhythm/Chord Charts	45757-2285-9
(Rhythm, Chord Charts, Drum Set and String Reduction)	
Soprano Rehearsal Track CD	45757-2286-0
Alto Rehearsal Track CD	45757-2286-5
Tenor Rehearsal Track CD	45757-2286-6
Bass Rehearsal Track CD	45757-2286-7
Drum Rehearsal Track CD	45757-2286-1
Bass Guitar Rehearsal Track CD	45757-2286-2
Guitar Rehearsal Track CD	45757-2286-3
Piano/Keyboard Rehearsal Track CD	45757-2286-4

INSTRUMENTATION:

Flute 1, 2
Oboe
Clarinet 1, 2
F Horn 1, 2 (Alto Sax)
Trumpet 1, 2
Trumpet 3

Trombone 1, 2
(Tenor Sax/Baritone T.C.)
Trombone 3/Tuba
Percussion
Violin 1, 2
Viola

Cello
Bass
Synth String Reduction
Rhythm
Drum Set
Chord Charts

www.christomlin.com • www.sixstepsrecords.com • www.brentwoodbenson.com

© 2013 sixstepsrecords, Sparrow Records®, in association with and manufactured by Brentwood-Benson Music Publications, 101 Winners Circle, Brentwood, TN 37027. All Rights Reserved. Unauthorized Duplication Prohibited.

 a division of

CONTENTS

Burning Lights (Instrumental) 3

Awake My Soul 5

Whom Shall I Fear (God of Angel Armies) 18

Lay Me Down 33

God's Great Dance Floor 48

White Flag 62

Crown Him (Majesty) 73

Jesus, Son of God 85

Sovereign 103

Countless Wonders 118

Thank You, God, for Saving Me 130

Shepherd Boy 144

Burning Lights
(Instrumental)

Words and Music by
CHRIS TOMLIN, DANIEL CARSON,
JASON INGRAM and JESSE REEVES
Arranged by Cliff Duren

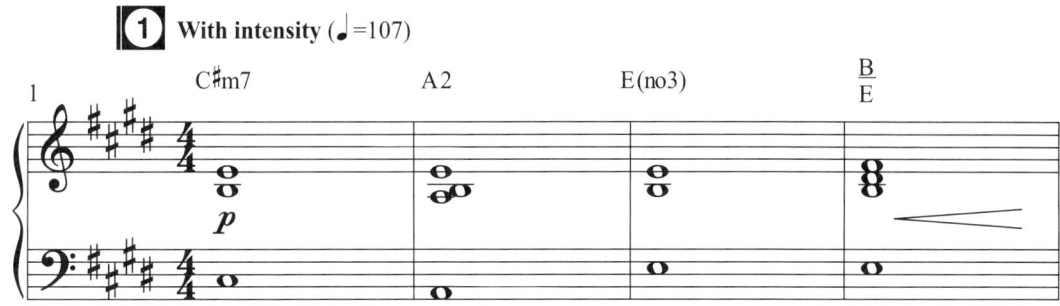

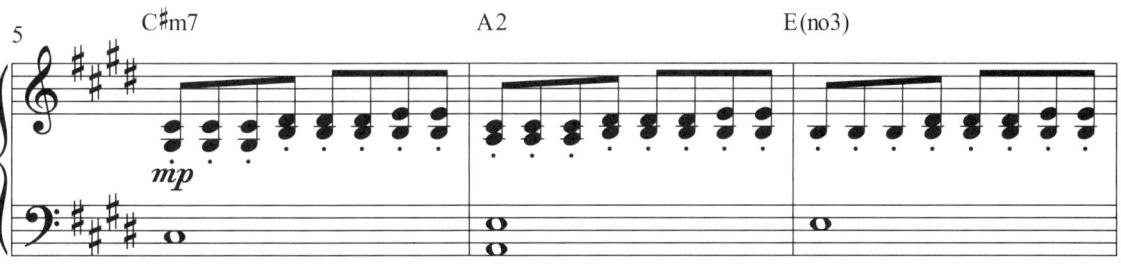

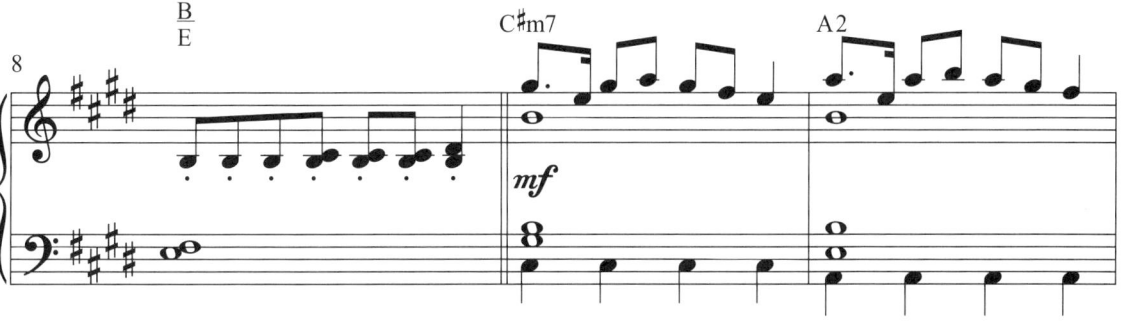

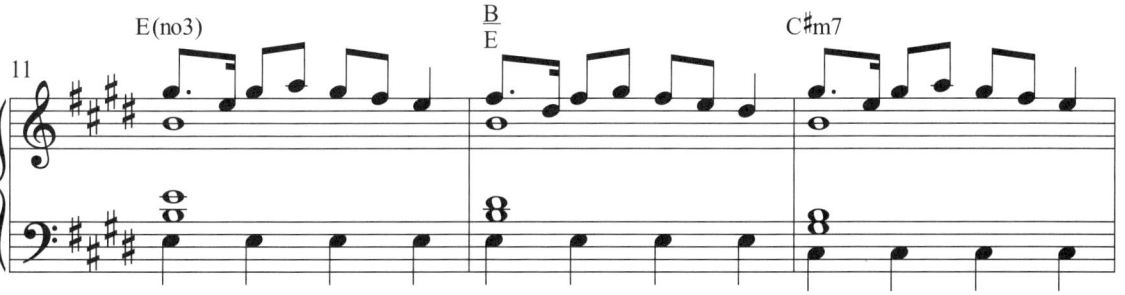

© Copyright 2013 (Arr. © Copyright 2013) worshiptogether.com Songs / sixsteps Music (ASCAP) / Worship Together Music / Sixsteps Songs / A Thousand Generations Publishing (BMI) (Administered at EMICMGPublishing.com) / Sony/ATV Music Publishing LLC / Open Hands Music (SESAC). Sony/ATV Music Publishing LLC / Open Hands Music administered by Sony/ATV Music Publishing LLC (8 Music Square West, Nashville, TN 37203). All rights reserved. Used by permission. *Reprinted by permission of Hal Leonard Corporation.*
PLEASE NOTE: Copying of this music is NOT covered by the CCLI license. For CCLI information call 1-800-234-2446.

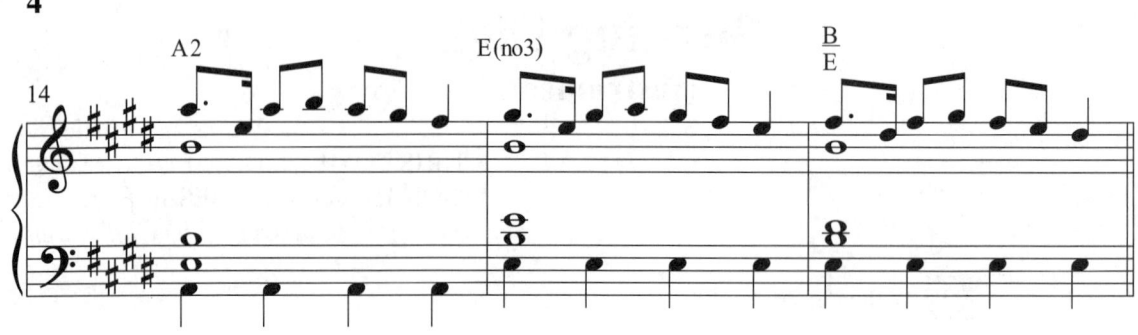
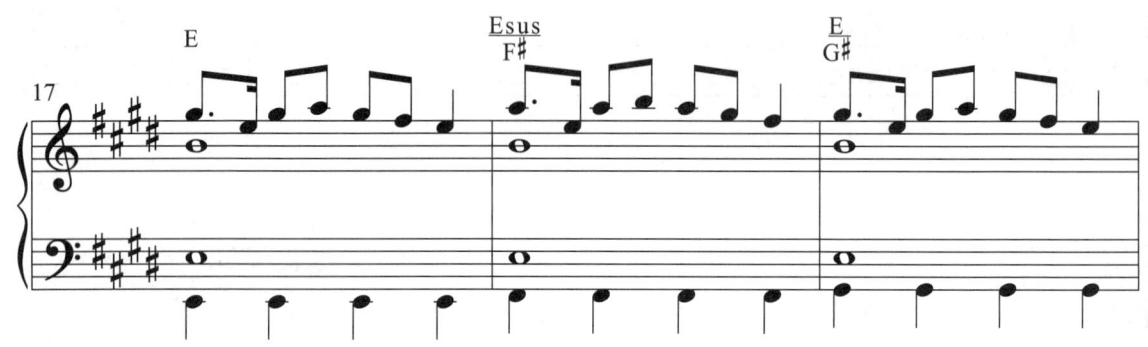
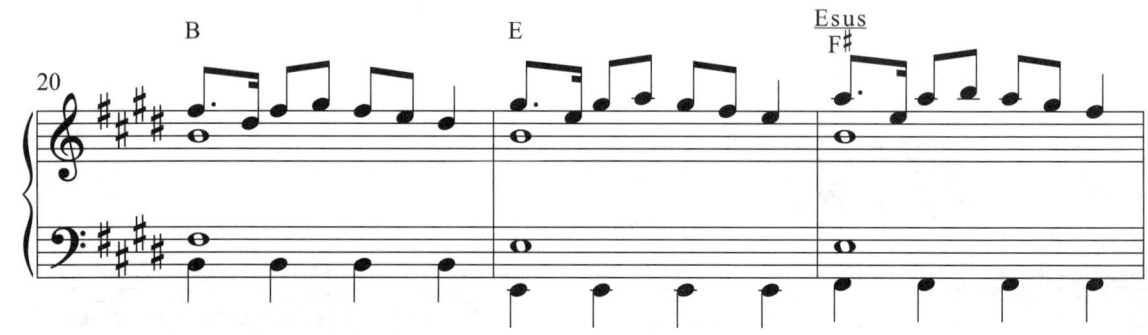
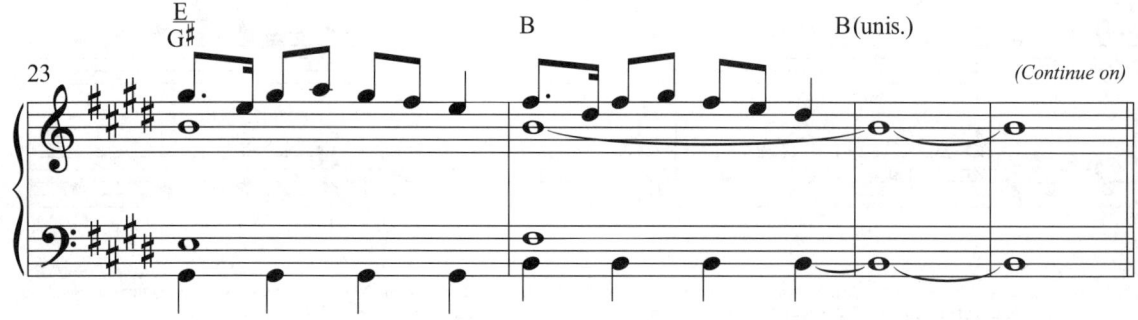

Awake My Soul

Words and Music by
CHRIS TOMLIN, DANIEL CARSON,
JASON INGRAM and JESSE REEVES
Arranged by Cliff Duren

© Copyright 2013 (Arr. © Copyright 2013) worshiptogether.com Songs / sixsteps Music (ASCAP) / Worship Together Music / Sixsteps Songs /
A Thousand Generations Publishing (BMI) (Administered at EMICMGPublishing.com) / Sony/ATV Music Publishing LLC /
Open Hands Music (SESAC). Sony/ATV Music Publishing LLC / Open Hands Music administered by Sony/ATV Music Publishing LLC
(8 Music Square West, Nashville, TN 37203). All rights reserved. Used by permission. *Reprinted by permission of Hal Leonard Corporation.*
PLEASE NOTE: Copying of this music is NOT covered by the CCLI license. For CCLI information call 1-800-234-2446.

SCRIPTURE READING:

[4] Then he said to me, "Prophesy to these bones and say to them, 'Dry bones, hear the word of the LORD! [5] This is what the Sovereign LORD says to these bones: I will make breath enter you, and you will come to life.'"

[7] So I prophesied as I was commanded. And as I was prophesying, there was a noise, a rattling sound, and the bones came together, bone to bone. [8] I looked, and tendons and flesh appeared on them and skin covered them, but there was no breath in them.

[9] Then he said to me, "Prophesy to the breath; prophesy, son of man, and say to it, … 'Come from the four winds, O breath, and breathe …'" *(Ezekiel 37:4,5,7-9a NIV)*

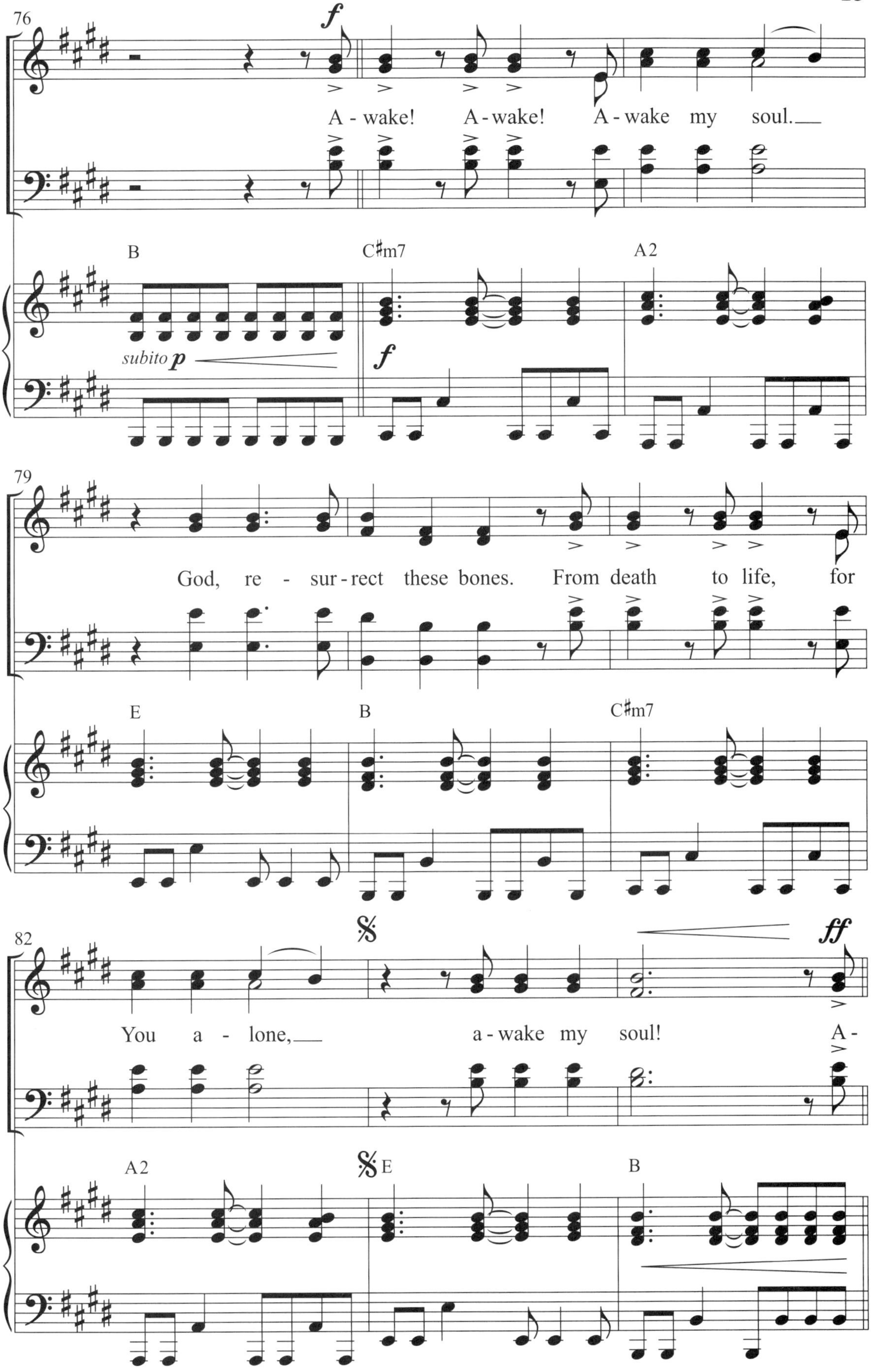
76
A - wake! A - wake! A - wake my soul.
B
C♯m7
A2
subito p
f
79
God, re - sur - rect these bones. From death to life, for
E
B
C♯m7
82
You a - lone, a - wake my soul! A -
ff
A2
E
B

Whom Shall I Fear
(God of Angel Armies)

Words and Music by
CHRIS TOMLIN, ED CASH
and SCOTT CASH
Arranged by Cliff Duren

You hear me when I call.   You are my morn-ing song.

© Copyright 2013 Worship Together Music / Sixsteps Songs / A Thousand Generations Publishing (BMI) (Administered at EMICMGPublishing.com) / Alletrop Music / McTyeire Music (Administered by Music Services). All rights reserved. Used by permission.
PLEASE NOTE: Copying of this music is NOT covered by the CCLI license. For CCLI information call 1-800-234-2446.

true: There's no life a-part from You. Lay me down. Lay me down. Lay me down.

Let-ting go of my pride, giv-ing up all my rights, take this life and let it shine, building

shine, shine!_ Take this life and let_ it shine!

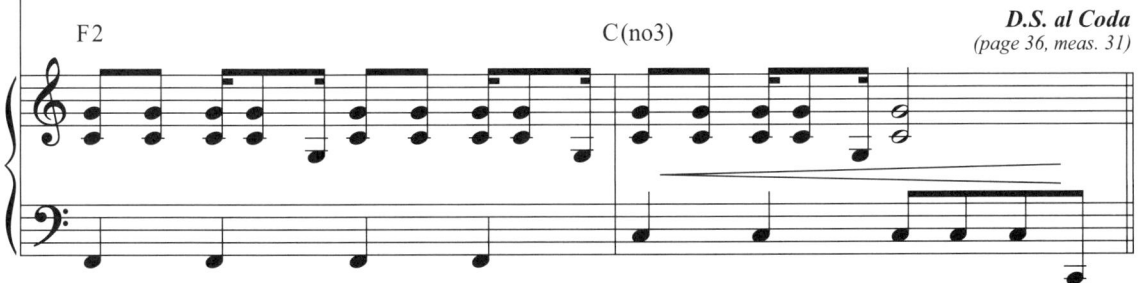

down. Woh! Lay me down. Lay me down. It will be my joy to say, "Your will. Your _way." It will be my joy to say,_ "Your _will. Your_ way." It will be my joy to say, "Your_ will. Your_ way, al-

-ways."

It will be my joy to say, "Your will. Your way." It will be my joy to say,

"Your will. Your way." It will be my joy to say, "Your will. Your way, always."

44

I lay me down. I'm not my own. I belong to You alone. Lay me down. Lay me down. Woh!

Hand on my heart. This much is true: There's no life a-part from You. Lay me down. Lay me down. Woh!

Lay me down. Lay me down. Woh!

Lay me down. Lay me down.

Lay me down! Lay me down!

47

God's Great Dance Floor

Words and Music by
CHRIS TOMLIN, MARTIN SMITH
and NICK HERBERT
Arranged by Cliff Duren

31 **Like a party** (♩=128)

I'm coming back to the start,

where You found me. I'm com-ing back to Your heart.

Now, I sur-ren-der. Take me.

This is all I can bring.

I'm com-ing back to the start. Our

God is free-dom. And here we feel Your heart, Your heart-beat for us. Take me. This is all I can bring. You'll nev-er stop lov-in' us no mat-ter how far we run!

You'll nev-er give up on us! All of heav-en shouts, "Let the fu-ture be-gin!"

Let the fu-ture be-gin!

Take me. This is

all__ I__ can bring.__ You'll nev-er stop lov-in' us no mat-ter how far we run! You'll nev-er give up on us! All of heav - en shouts, "Let the fu - ture be - gin!" You'll

nev - er stop lov-in' us no mat-ter how far we run!

unis.
You'll nev-er give up on us! All of
unis.

heav-en shouts, "Let the fu-ture be-gin!"

Let the fu-ture be-gin!

I feel a-live! I come a-live!

I am a-live on God's great dance floor! I feel a-live!

I come a-live! I am a-live on God's great dance floor!

On God's great dance floor!

I feel a-live! I come a-live!

I am a-live on God's great dance floor! I feel a-live!

I come a-live! I am a-live on God's great dance floor!

Woh! Woh! Woh! Woh! Woh! Woh! On God's great dance floor! Woh! Woh! Woh! Woh! Woh! Woh! On God's great dance floor!

Woh! Woh! Woh! Woh! Woh! Woh! On God's great dance floor! Woh! Woh! Woh! Woh! Woh! Woh! On God's great dance floor!

White Flag

Words and Music by
CHRIS TOMLIN, JASON INGRAM,
MATT MAHER and MATT REDMAN
Arranged by Cliff Duren

39 With intensity (♩=82)

WORSHIP LEADER (Male)

The bat-tle rag-es on,

as storm and tem-pest roar.

© Copyright 2012 (Arr. © Copyright 2013) Thankyou Music (PRS) (Administered worldwide at EMICMGPublishing.com excluding Europe which is administered by kingswaysongs) / worshiptogether.com Songs / sixsteps Music / Said and Done Music (ASCAP) / Worship Together Music / Sixsteps Songs / A Thousand Generations Publishing / Valley of Songs Music (BMI) (Administered at EMICMGPublishing.com) / Sony/ATV Music Publishing LLC / West Main Music / Windsor Hill Music (SESAC). Sony/ATV Music Publishing LLC / West Main Music / Windsor Hill Music administered by Sony/ATV Music Publishing LLC (8 Music Square West, Nashville, TN 37203).
All rights reserved. Used by permission. *Reprinted by permission of Hal Leonard Corporation.*
PLEASE NOTE: Copying of this music is NOT covered by the CCLI license. For CCLI information call 1-800-234-2446.

We can-not win this fight _inside our reb-el hearts._ This

building

free-dom song is march-ing on.

64 *CHOIR*

We raise our white flag. We sur-ren-der all to You, all for You. We raise our white flag. The war is o-ver. Love has come. Your love has won.

Here on this holy ground,

You made a way for peace.

Laying Your body down,

66

You took our rightful place.

42 *building*

We're laying down our weapons now.

G(no3)   F2   Am7   G/B   C

building

f *unis.*

We raise our white flag. We surrender all to You,

mel. unis.

Am7   F2   C   G(no3)   Am7   F2

f

all for You. We raise our white flag. The war is o - ver.
Love has come. Your love has won!

We

lift the cross. Lift it high. Lift it high. We lift the cross. Lift it

building

high. Lift it high. We lift the cross. Lift it high. Lift it high. We

mel. **f**

lift the cross. Lift it high. Lift it high. We lift the cross! Lift it

56
high! Lift it high! We lift the cross! Lift ___ it high! Lift it high! We
C(no3) G C/E F2 C(no3) G
59
45
lift the cross! Lift ___ it high! Lift it high! We lift the cross! Lift ___ it
C/E F2 C(no3) G C/E F2
f
62
mf unis.
high! Lift it high! We raise our white flag. We sur-ren - der
mel. unis.
C(no3) G Am7 F2 C(no3) G(no3)
subito p

all to You, all for You. We raise our white flag.

The war is o-ver. Love has come. Your love has won!

We raise our white flag. We sur-ren-der all to You,

all for You. We raise our white flag. The war is o - ver.

Love has come. Your love has won! We lift the cross! Lift it high! Lift it high! We lift the cross! Lift it high! Lift it high! We lift the cross! Lift it

high! Lift it high! We lift the cross! Lift it

high! Lift it high!

Crown Him
(Majesty)

Words by
MATTHEW BRIDGES
and GODFREY THRING

Music by
GEORGE J. ELVEY
New Words and Music by
CHRIS TOMLIN, ED CASH
and MATT MAHER
Arranged by Cliff Duren

F♯m E D A/C♯ A G G2(♯4) G2 D/F♯ E/G♯
mp
48
A little faster (♩=75)
F♯m7 D2 A/C♯ Esus E
mp
SOLO (Female)
mp
Crown Him with man - y crowns; the Lamb up - on the
F♯m7 D2 A/C♯
mp
throne. Hark! How the heav - 'nly an - them drowns all
Esus E F♯m A/E B/D♯ E

music but its own. A - wake my soul and sing of Him who died for me. And hail Him as thy matchless King through all e-ter-ni-ty.

CHOIR and SOLOIST

Maj - es - ty! Lord of all! Let ev - 'ry throne be- fore Him fall! The King of kings! Oh, come a - dore our God who reigns for - ev - er-

more! Crown Him the Lord of life who tri-umphed o'er the grave, and rose vic-to-rious in the strife for those He came to save. His glories now we sing who died and rose on high; who died eternal life to bring and lives that death may die.

Maj - es - ty! Lord of all! Let ev - 'ry throne be - fore Him fall! The King of kings! Oh, come a - dore our God who reigns for - ev - er-

more! For-ev-er-more! All hail, Re-deem-er, hail, for He has died for me! His praise and glo-ry shall not fail through-

out eter-nity! All hail, Re-deem-er, hail, for He has died for me! His praise and glo-ry shall not fail throughout eter - ni - ty!

Maj - es - ty! Lord of all! Let ev - 'ry throne be-fore Him fall! The King of kings! Oh, come a-dore our God who reigns for-ev-er-more! Majesty! Lord of all! Let ev-'ry throne be-fore Him fall! The King of kings! Oh,

56
106
come a-dore our God who reigns for - ev - er-more! Praise
Bmaj7/D♯ B/D♯ Bsus/C♯ B/D♯ F♯sus B
109
God who reigns for - ev - er - more! You're the
Bsus/C♯ B/D♯ F♯sus B B/D♯
111
molto rit.
God who reigns for - ev - er-more!
Bsus/C♯ B/D♯ F♯sus B
molto rit.

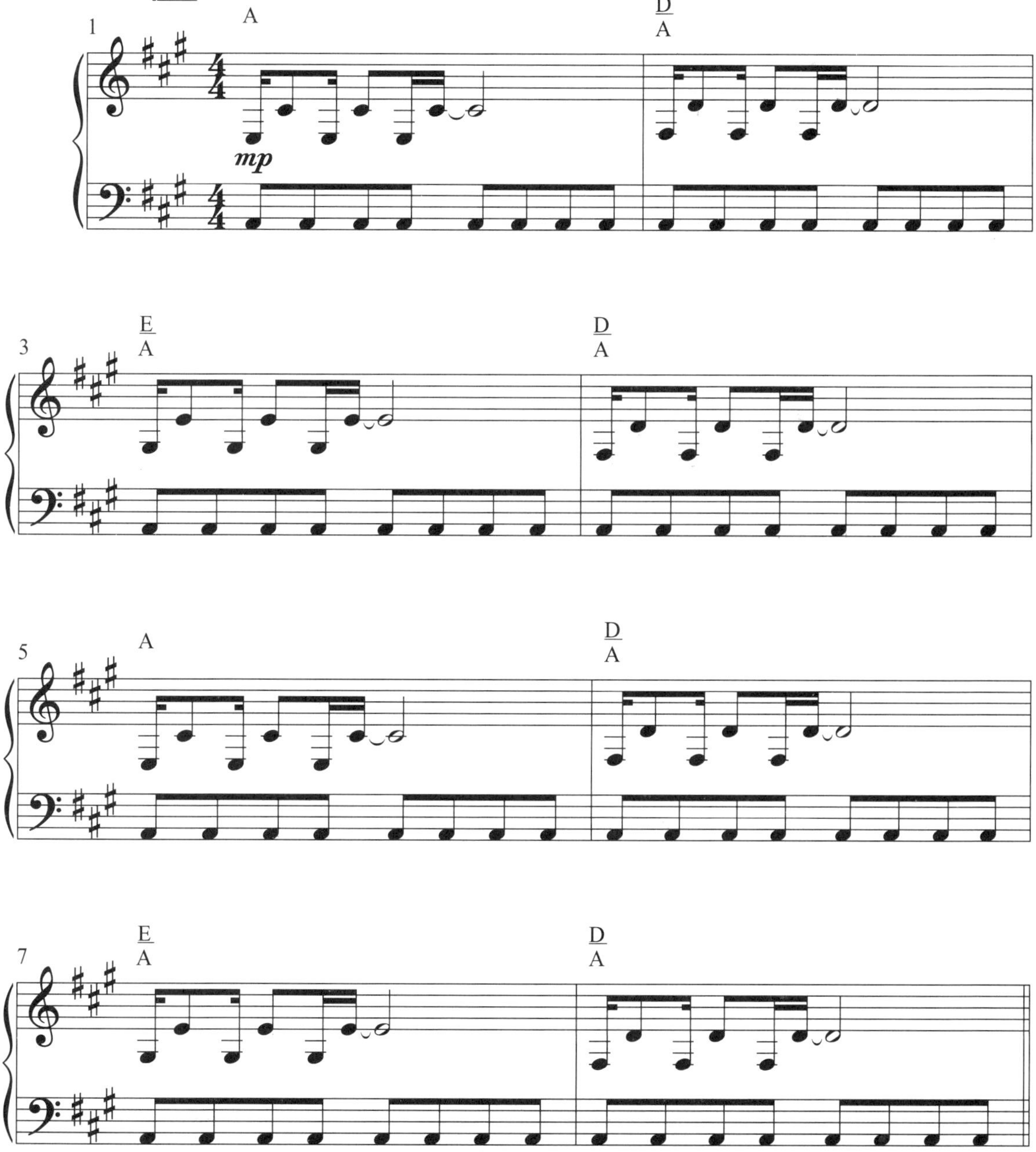

86

SOLO (Female)

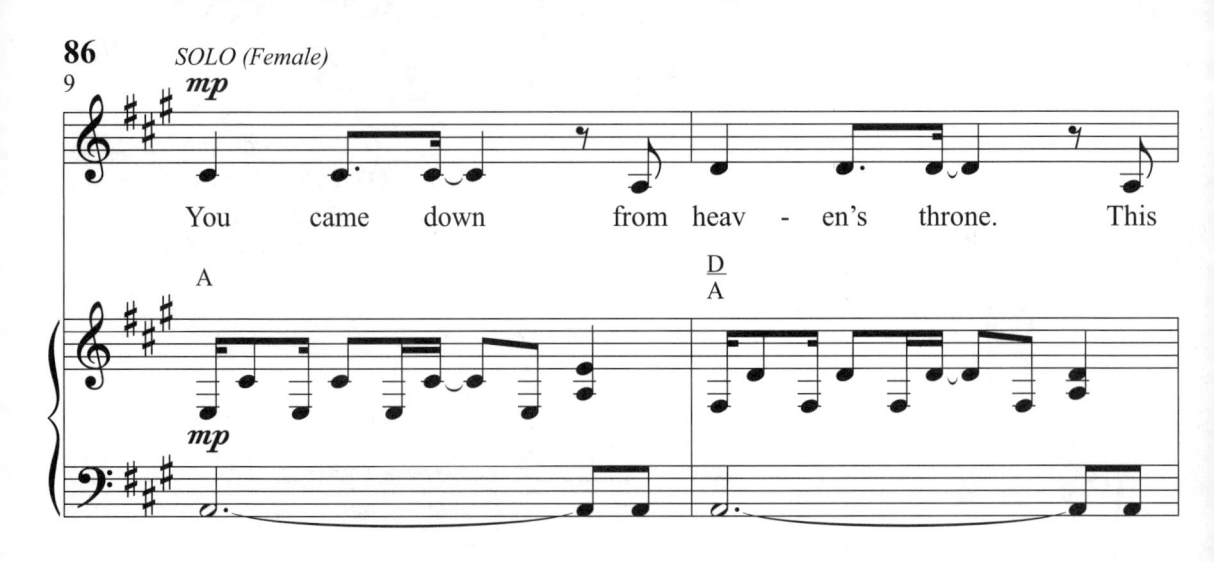

You came down from heav-en's throne. This earth You formed was not Your home. A love like this the world had nev-er known.

crown of thorns to mock Your name. For-
giveness fell upon Your face. A

love like this the world had nev-er known.

end SOLO

CHOIR and WORSHIP LEADER

On the al-tar of our praise, let there be no high-er name:

Je - sus, Son of God. You laid down Your per - fect life. You are the sac - ri - fice. Je - sus, Son of God. You are

Je - sus, Son___ of God.___ You took our sin. You bore our shame. You rose to life. You de-feat-ed___ the grave. A

91

love like this the world has nev-er known.

took our sin. You bore our shame. You

You

F#m7 D A(no3) A Asus/B

building

f

mel.

fp building

45
rose to life. You de - feat - ed the grave. A
A/C♯
D
47
love like this the world has nev - er known.
unis.
A/E
D/F♯
62
49
f
On the
A/C♯
D2
E(no3)

al - tar of our praise, let there be no high - er name: Je - sus, Son of God. You laid down Your per - fect life. You are the sac - ri - fice.

Je - sus, Son of God. You are
Je - sus, Son of God. Be lift - ed
high - er than all You've o - ver - come. Your name be

loud - er than an - y oth - er song. There is no pow - er that can come a - gainst Your love. The cross was e - nough. The cross was e - nough. Be lift - ed

D2　　　　　　　　　　A　　　E(no3)

D2/F#　　　　　　　A/C#　　　E(no3)

D2　　　　A/C#　　　F#m7　　　E(no3)

high - er than all You've o - ver - come. Your name be loud - er than an - y oth - er song. There is no pow - er that can come a - gainst Your love. The

D2   A   E(no3)
D2   A   E(no3)
D2/F#   A/C#   E(no3)

for Alternate version, jump to 𝄋
(page 102, meas. 114)

cross was e-nough. The cross was e-nough. The

cross was e-nough. The cross was e-nough.

On the al-tar of our praise, let there

be no high-er name: Je-sus, Son of God. You laid down Your per-fect life. You are the sac-ri-fice. Je-sus, Son of God. You are Je-sus, Son of God.

WORSHIP LEADER: The Word of God says, "Christ Jesus: being in very nature God, did not consider equality with God something to be used to his own advantage; rather, he made himself nothing ... humbled himself, becoming obedient to death — even death on a cross! Therefore God exalted him to the highest place and gave him the name that is above every name."   *(taken from Philippians 2:6-9 NIV)*

Be lift - ed

high - er than all You've o - ver-come. Your name be louder than any other song. There is no power that can come against Your love. The

cross was e-nough. The cross was e-nough. Be lift-ed
higher than all You've o-ver-come. Your name be
louder than any other song. There is no

power that can come a-gainst Your love. The cross was e-nough. The cross was e-nough. The cross was e-nough. The cross was e-nough.

Sovereign

Words and Music by
CHRIS TOMLIN, JASON INGRAM,
JONAS MYRIN, MARTIN CHALK
and MATT REDMAN
Arranged by Cliff Duren

© Copyright 2013 (Arr. © Copyright 2013) Shout! Publishing (APRA) (Administered in the US and Canada at EMICMGPublishing.com) / Thankyou Music (PRS) (Administered worldwide at EMICMGPublishing.com excluding Europe which is administered by Kingswaysongs) / worshiptogether.com Songs / sixsteps Music / Said and Done Music (ASCAP) / Worship Together Music / Sixsteps Songs / A Thousand Generations Publishing (BMI) (Administered at EMICMGPublishing.com) / Sony/ATV Music Publishing LLC / Open Hands Music (SESAC) / Martin Chalk Music. Sony/ATV Music Publishing LLC / Open Hands Music administered by Sony/ATV Music Publishing LLC (8 Music Square West, Nashville, TN 37203). All rights reserved. Used by permission. *Reprinted by permission of Hal Leonard Corporation.*
PLEASE NOTE: Copying of this music is NOT covered by the CCLI license. For CCLI information call 1-800-234-2446.

CHOIR

Sov-'reign in the moun-tain air. Sov-'reign on the o-cean floor.

D(no3)   Bm7

With me in the calm, with me in the storm.

G2   Bm7   A(no3)

Sov-'reign in my great-est joy. Sov-'reign in my deep-est cry.

D(no3)   Bm7

With me in the dark, with me at the dawn.

In Your ev-er-last-ing arms,— all the piec-es of my life. From be-gin-ning to the end, I can trust You.

In Your nev-er-fail-ing love, You work ev-'ry-thing for good. God, what-ev-er comes my way, I will trust You. Sov-'reign in the moun-tain air.

Sov-'reign on the o-cean floor. With me in the calm,

Bm7   G2

with me in the storm. Sov-'reign in my great-est joy.

Bm7   A(no3)   D(no3)

Sov-'reign in my deep-est cry. With me in the dark,

Bm7   G2

108

with me at the dawn. In Your ev-er-last-ing arms,

Bm7   A(no3)   D(no3)

all the piec-es of my life. From be-gin-ning to the

Bm7   G2

end, I can trust You. In Your nev-er-fail-ing love,

Bm7   A(no3)   D(no3)

unis.

You work ev-'ry-thing for good. God, what-ev-er comes my

Bm7   G2

way, I will trust You. God, what-ev-er comes my

Bm7   A(no3)   G2

way, I will trust You. All my hopes, all I

Bm7   A(no3)   D/F#   G2

mp unis.

subito p

110

Lyrics:
need, held in Your hands! All my life, all of me held in Your hands! All my fears, all my dreams held in Your hands!

All my hopes, all I need, held in Your hands!

All my life, all of me held in Your hands!

All my fears, all my dreams held in Your hands!

112

In Your ev-er-last-ing arms, all the piec-es of my life. From be-gin-ning to the end, I can trust You.

In Your nev-er-fail-ing love, You work ev-'ry-thing for good. God, what-ev-er comes my way, I will trust You. In Your ev-er-last-ing arms, all the piec-es of my life. From be-gin-ning to the end, I can trust You. In Your nev-er-fail-ing love, You work ev-'ry-thing for good. God, what-ev-er comes my way, I will trust You.

God, what-ev-er comes my way, I will trust You.

God, what-ev-er comes my way, I will trust You.

73 OPTIONAL NARRATIVE TAG

SCRIPTURE READING:

Those who know your name will trust in you, for you, LORD, have never forsaken those who seek you. *(Psalm 9:10 NIV)*

But I trust in your unfailing love; my heart rejoices in your salvation. *(Psalm 13:5 NIV)*

In you, LORD my God, I put my trust. *(Psalm 25:1 NIV)*

When I am afraid, I put my trust in you. *(Psalm 56:3 NIV)*

LORD Almighty, blessed is the one who trusts in you. *(Psalm 84:12 NIV)*

Let the morning bring me word of your unfailing love, for I have put my trust in you. Show me the way I should go, for to you I entrust my life. *(Psalm 143:8 NIV)*

Your kingdom is an everlasting kingdom, and your dominion endures through all generations. The LORD is trustworthy in all he promises and faithful in all he does.

(Psalm 145:13 NIV)

117

(page 116, meas. 92)

I will trust___ You.

I will trust___ You.

Countless Wonders

Words and Music by
CHRIS TOMLIN, ED CASH
and MATT ARMSTRONG
Arranged by Cliff Duren

[75] Pop groove (♩=80)

SOLO (Female)

You reign in end-less pow-er a-bove the world You made.

A-cross the sky is writ-ten Your maj-es-ty and praise.

And still, You move in mer-cy and heal the hum-ble heart.

© Copyright 2013 Worship Together Music / Sixsteps Songs / A Thousand Generations Publishing (BMI) (Administered at EMICMGPublishing.com) / Universal Music - Brentwood Benson Tunes / Fots Music / Countless Wonder Publishing (SESAC) / Universal Music - Brentwood Benson Songs / McKittrick Music (BMI) (Licensing through Music Services). All rights reserved. Used by permission.
PLEASE NOTE: Copying of this music is NOT covered by the CCLI license. For CCLI information call 1-800-234-2446.

For ev-'ry soul that's search-ing, Je-sus, there You are.

CHOIR and SOLOIST

Your beau-ty fills the skies! Your glo-ry reigns in bril-liant light! Great God of count-less won-ders,

I will lift my ___ eyes. Your beauty fills the skies!

Your glory reigns in brilliant light! Great God of countless wonders,

I will lift my ___ eyes. ___

I will lift my eyes.

The mys-ter-ies of heav-en and all Your works dis-played— ev-'ry star, ev-'ry o-

-cean the uni-verse pro-claims. For ev-'ry sun that ris-es, Your faith-ful-ness to me— like the chang-ing of the sea-sons, like the riv-er to the sea, yeah!

Your beau-ty fills the skies! Your glo-ry reigns in bril-liant light!

E♭   E♭/F

Great God of count-less won-ders, I will lift my eyes.

Cm7   E♭/A♭

Your beau-ty fills the skies! Your glo-ry reigns in bril-liant light!

E♭   E♭/F

Great God of count-less won - ders, I will lift my eyes.

No one can fath - om all Your might - y works, O God. Just one glimpse of You and I am o-ver-come. You o-pen up Your hand

Cm7   B♭(no3)   A♭2   E♭(no3)

and pour out, once a-gain, Your ev - er-last - ing love.

Cm7   B♭(no3)   A♭2   E♭(no3)

SOLO
mf

Your beau-ty fills the skies!

B♭(no3)   E♭

mf

126

(81)

Your glo-ry reigns in bril-liant light! Great God of count-less won-ders,

E♭sus/F   Cm7

CHOIR and SOLOIST (with more freedom)
f

I will lift my eyes. Your beau-ty fills the skies!

E♭/A♭   E♭

Your glo-ry reigns in bril-liant light! Great God of count-less won-ders,

E♭/F   Cm7

I will lift my eyes. Your beauty fills the skies!

Your glory reigns in brilliant light! Great God of countless wonders,

I will lift my eyes. Your beauty fills the skies!

128

Your glo-ry reigns in bril-liant light! Great God of count-less won-ders,

E♭/F   Cm7

82

I will lift my eyes.

E♭/A♭   E♭

I will lift my eyes.

E♭/F   Cm7

129

I will lift my eyes.

I will lift my eyes.

I will lift my eyes.

Thank You, God, for Saving Me

Words and Music by
CHRIS TOMLIN
and PHIL WICKHAM
Arranged by Cliff Duren

83 Relaxed groove (♩=88)

SOLO (Female)
What can I give to You? What can I offer to___ a King? For all_ the love You've shown,

SOLO (Male)

© Copyright 2013 Worship Together Music / Sixsteps Songs / A Thousand Generations Publishing (BMI)
(Administered at EMICMGPublishing.com) / Phil Wickham Music / Seems Like Music
(Both administered by Simpleville Publishing, LLC). All rights reserved. Used by permission.
PLEASE NOTE: Copying of this music is NOT covered by the CCLI license. For CCLI information call 1-800-234-2446.

131

for all Your mer-cy o - ver me.

E♭   B♭   Cm7

DUET

I called Your name. You heard my cry.

A♭2

Out of the grave and in-to life.

E♭   A♭2

My heart is Yours. My soul is free.

Cm7   Ab2   Eb/G

Thank You, God, for sav - ing me.

Eb   Ebsus

CHOIR
mp

Thank You, God, for sav - ing me. The Rock of sal-

Eb   Ebsus

25
va - tion; my hope is built on noth - ing less.
A♭2 E♭ B♭
mp
28
Morn - ing by morn - ing, how great
Cm7 A♭2 E♭
31
85
is Your faith - ful - ness.
mf
I called Your name.
mel.
B♭ Cm7

You heard my cry. Out of the grave and in-to life. My heart is Yours. My soul is free.

Thank You, God, for saving me.

Thank You, God, for saving me.

Thank You, God, for saving me.

136

DUET ad libs

Ooo___ Ooo___ Thank You, God, for sav-ing me.___ Thank You,

CHOIR
Ooo___

Chords: E♭ | E♭sus | E♭ | E♭sus

137

Lord.____ Thank You, God.

Thank You, God, for sav - ing me!____

E♭   E♭sus

87

Thank You, God, for sav - ing me!____

E♭   E♭sus

138

DUET

You gave Your life upon the cross. You suf-fered once for all! You made a way! Je-sus, in vic-to-ry You rose! You made us all Your own! Now, we are saved!

CHOIR and DUET

You gave Your life up-on the cross. You suf-fered once for all! You made a way!

Je - sus, in vic - to - ry You rose! You made us all Your own! Now, we are saved!

Thank You, God, for sav - ing me!

SOLO (Male) ad lib

141

Thank You, God, for sav - ing me!

Thank You, God, for sav - ing me,____ for sav-

- ing me!

I called Your name. You heard my cry. Out of the grave and into life. My heart is Yours. My soul is free.

143

Thank You, God, for sav-ing me. Thank You, God, for sav-ing me. Thank You, God, for sav-ing me. Thank You, God, for sav-ing me.

E♭   E♭sus   E♭   E♭sus   E♭   E♭sus   E♭   E♭sus   E♭

Shepherd Boy

**Words and Music by
CHRIS TOMLIN and MARTIN SMITH**
Arranged by Cliff Duren

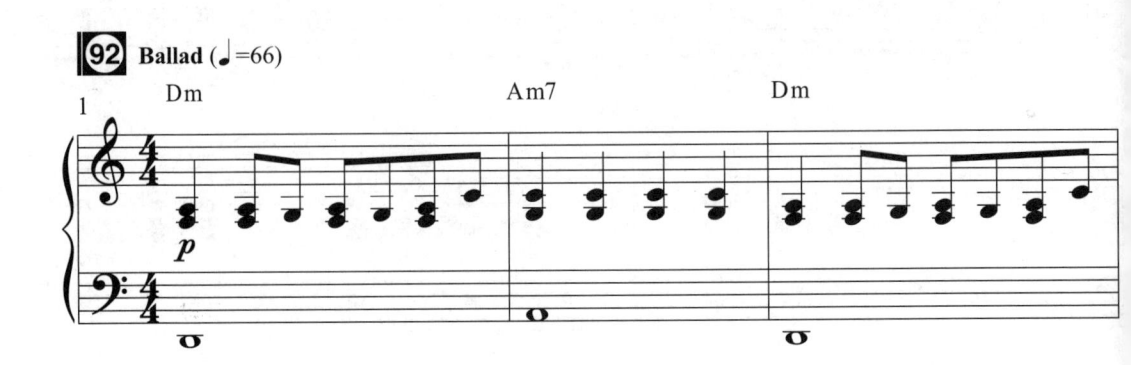

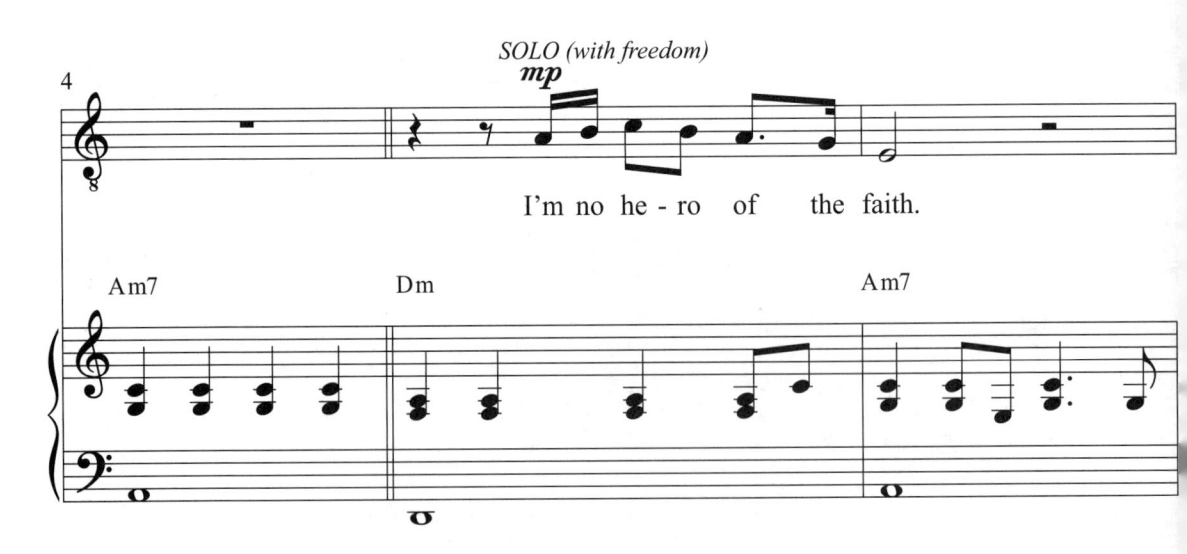

Ballad (♩=66)

I'm no he-ro of the faith.

I'm not as strong as I once thought I was. I'm just a

© Copyright 2013 Thankyou Music (PRS) (Administered worldwide at EMICMGPublishing.com excluding Europe which is administered by Kingswaysongs) / Worship Together Music / Sixsteps Songs / A Thousand Generations Publishing (BMI) / Gloworks (PRS) (Administered at EMICMGPublishing.com). All rights reserved. Used by permission.
PLEASE NOTE: Copying of this music is NOT covered by the CCLI license. For CCLI information call 1-800-234-2446.

Shep - herd Boy, sing-ing to a choir of burn - ing lights.

I'm just sing - in', sing-in' o - ver you.

Come and lay your trou - bles down,

'cause love is break - in' through.

I was born to lift a song of hope, see the heav-ens o-pen up. Take this ar-mor; lest I die. Take this crown and let me fly. I'm just

building

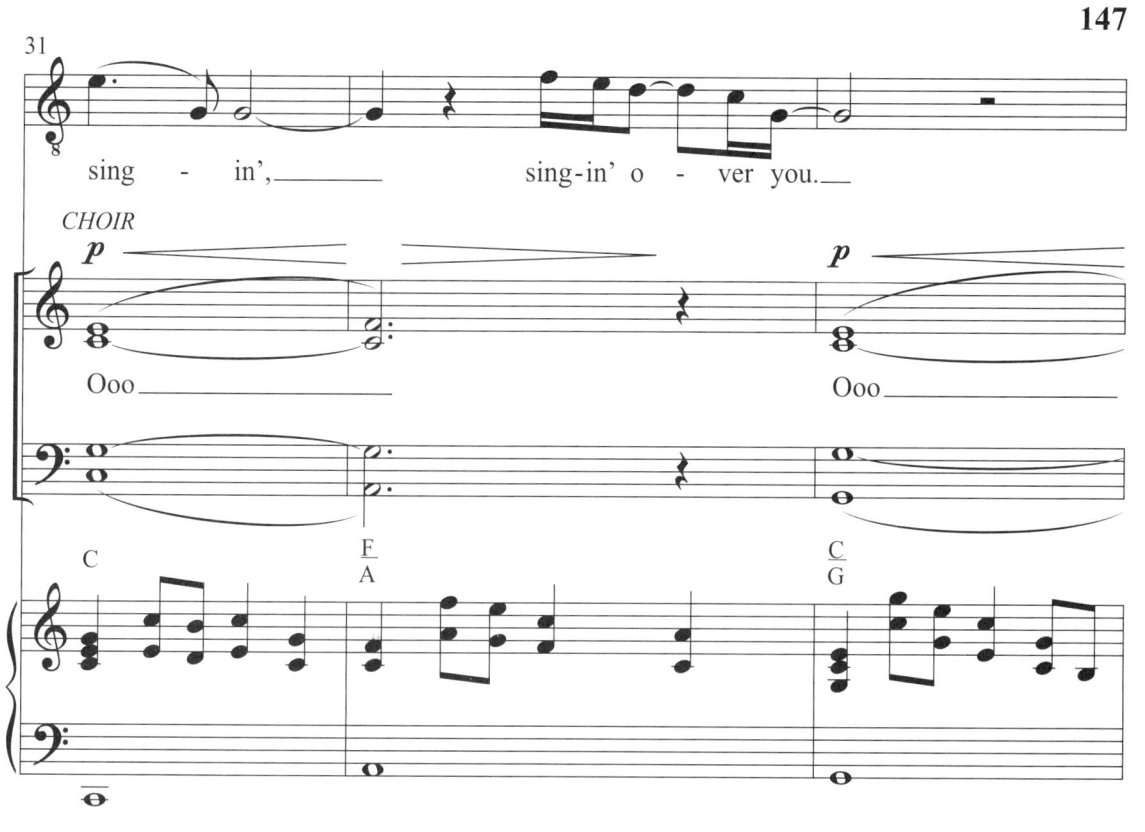

sing - in',_____ sing-in' o - ver you.___

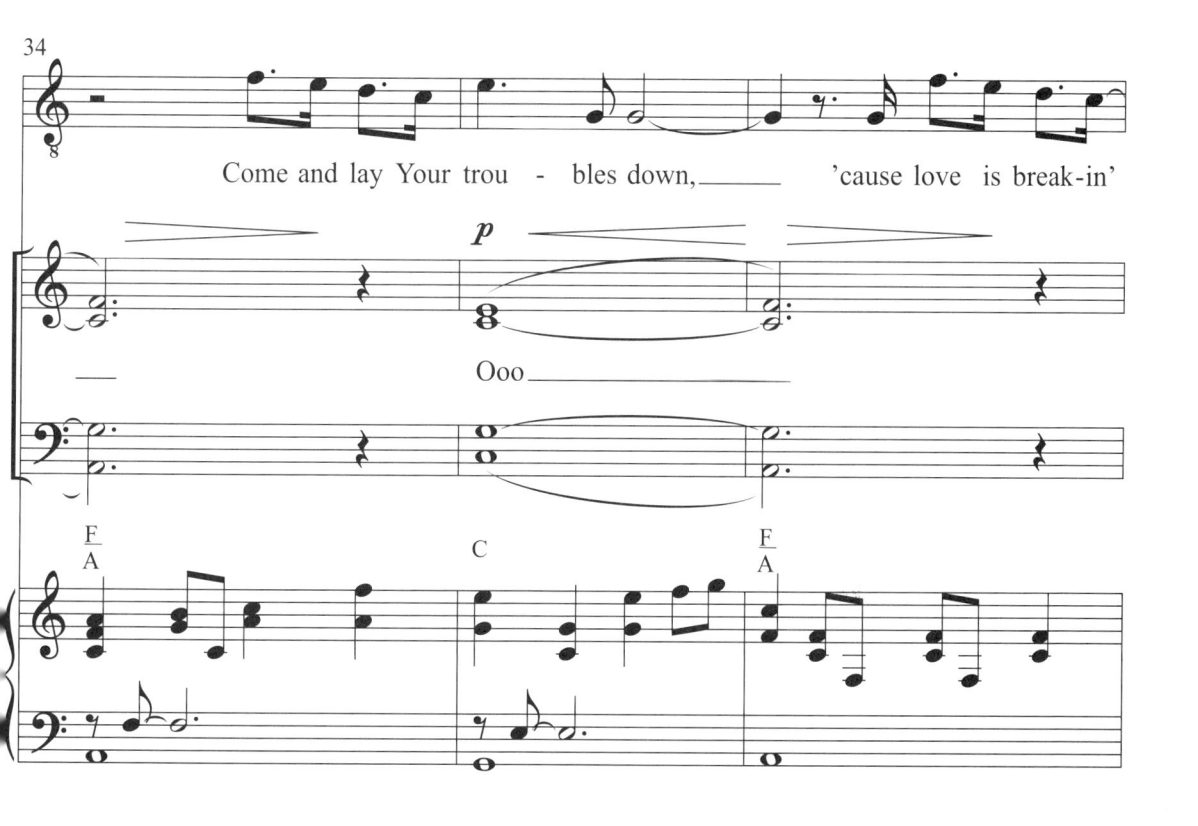

CHOIR
Ooo_____ Ooo_____

Come and lay Your trou - bles down,_____ 'cause love is break-in'

Ooo_____

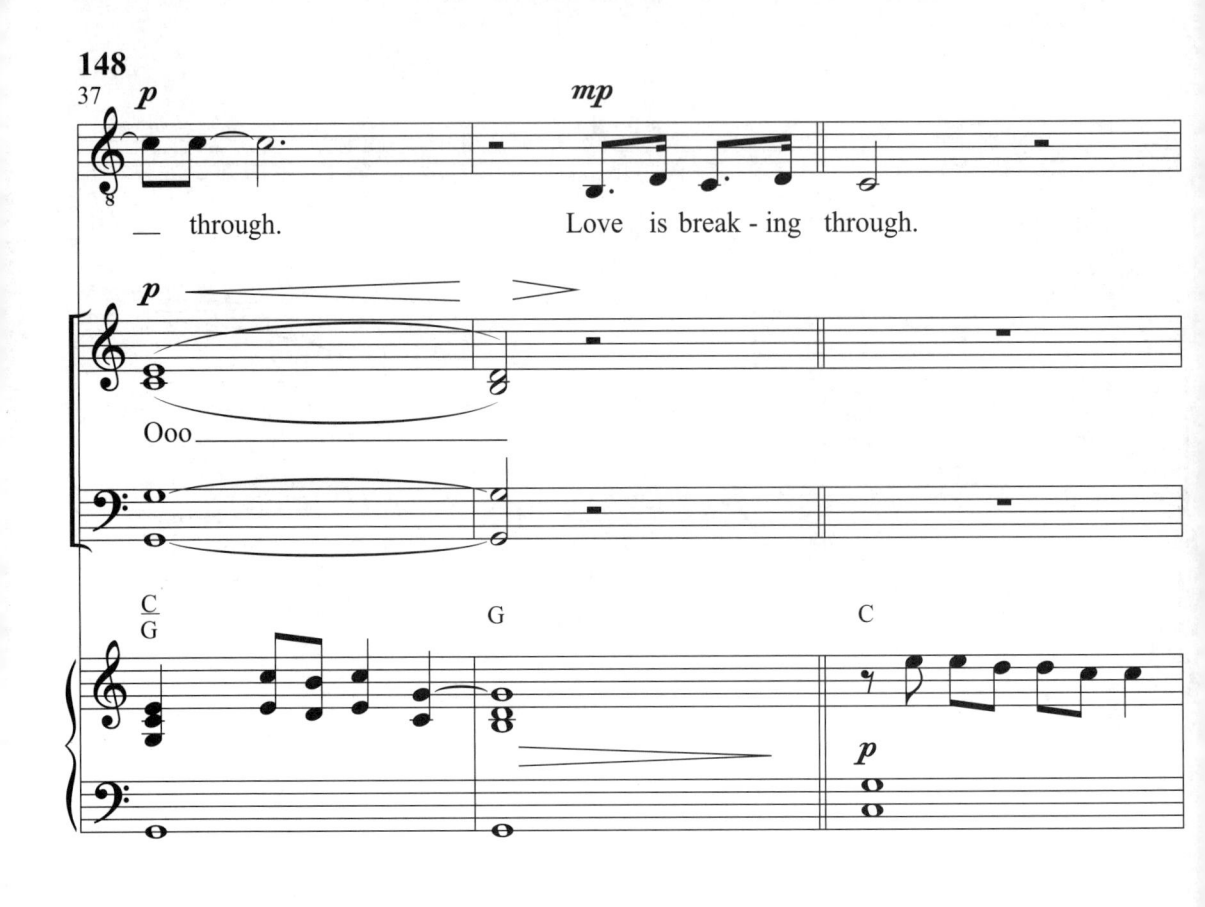

through. Love is break-ing through.

Ooo

We're just sing - in', sing-in' out to You.

Our hearts are Yours for - ev - er.

Your love is break - in' through.

We're just sing - in', sing-in' out to You.

Our hearts are Yours for - ev - er.

Your love is break - in' through.

62
ff
Love
is a fire!
unis.
G
C
ff
F
A
65
Love
is a fire!
unis.
Love
C
F
A
F
C
68
97
mp
unis.
is a fire!
unis.
We're just
opt. Tenor only
F
A
C
F
A

sing - in', sing-in' out to You.

Our hearts are Yours for - ev - er. Your love is break-in' through.

Love is break - ing through.